Embracing Our Queenly Anointing

Anointed for Such a Time as This

Esther 4:14

Dr. Sharon Smith

Workbook

Created in 2019 by Inspired Wholeness Ministries

Inspired
Wholeness Ministries

How to Use Workbook

"Embracing Our Queenly Anointing" as a Bible study course should be utilized to gain a better understanding of the book of Esther, in an effort to bring the women studying, to a place of knowing, and therefore embracing their anointing as Queens in God's royal kingdom. The study should help the women understand that no matter what they have had to endure; God's plan is to embrace them as royalty. This Workbook should be used in conjunction with "Embracing Our Queenly Anointing" course book. After reading the course book in its entirety the students/Bible study participants are asked to complete each lesson. Each lesson asks the students/Bible study participants to answer five crucial questions that when answered honestly has the potential to bring wholeness and the freedom to accept their anointing and walk in it with boldness and tenacity.

Lesson 1

Esther 1:1-22 = Read this portion of Vashti that is written in the back of the Course book

- **Read <u>Being Deposed as Queen</u> in the Course book:**

   1. **Do you think Vashti was a bad queen? Why/Why not?**

   _____

   _____

   _____

   _____

   _____

   _____

   _____

   _____

   _____

   _____

   _____

   _____

   _____

   2. **How are you being groomed for certain positions in your ministry/church?**

   _____

   _____

   _____

   _____

   _____

   _____

   _____

   _____

   _____

   _____

   _____

   _____

   _____

   _____

3. What does Vashti's refusal say about her integrity?

_____

_____

_____

_____

_____

_____

_____

_____

_____

_____

_____

_____

4. Why does God sometimes have to remove family members from our lives to move us into our royal positions?

_____

_____

_____

_____

_____

_____

_____

_____

_____

_____

_____

_____

_____

5. **How can you identify with Vashti?**

_____

_____

_____

_____

_____

_____

_____

_____

_____

_____

_____

_____

Lesson 2

Esther 2:8-15 = Read this portion of Esther that is written in the back of the Course book

- **Read <u>Preparing for Our Royal Lineage</u> in the Course book:**

  1. **Has God given you a specific assignment in your ministry/church? If so what?**

  _____

  _____

  _____

  _____

  _____

  _____

  _____

  _____

  _____

  _____

  _____

  _____

  _____

  _____

  _____

  1. **How are you being prepared for your assignment?**

  _____

  _____

  _____

  _____

  _____

  _____

  _____

  _____

  _____

  _____

  _____

2. How can your preparation and anointing rescue a certain people from doom?

_____

_____

_____

_____

_____

_____

_____

_____

_____

3. What specific make-over treatments has God put in place so you can be ready for your assignment?

_____

_____

_____

_____

_____

_____

_____

_____

_____

4. **What oils and perfumes of life have you had to encounter in an effort to prepare for your meeting with the King? How have you dealt with, or are you dealing with the difficult oils/perfumes?**

_____

_____

_____

_____

_____

_____

_____

_____

_____

_____

_____

_____

<u>Lesson 3</u>

Esther 2:5-7 = Read this portion of Esther that is written in the back of the Course book

- **Read <u>Walking in the Meaning of Our Name</u> in the Course book:**

    1. **What is your name? Do you know the meaning of your name? If yes write it here. If not look up the meaning and write it here.**

    _____

    _____

    _____

    _____

    _____

    _____

    _____

    _____

    _____

    _____

    _____

    _____

    _____

    2. **What kind of things does the meaning of your name conjure up in your mind?**

    _____

    _____

    _____

    _____

    _____

    _____

    _____

    _____

    _____

    _____

    _____

    _____

3. How can you utilize the meaning of your name (if the name is positive), or the opposite meaning of your name (if the name is negative) to accomplish your anointing?

_____

_____

_____

_____

_____

_____

_____

_____

_____

_____

_____

4. How are you invoking greatness whether your name meaning is positive or negative?

_____

_____

_____

_____

_____

_____

_____

_____

_____

_____

_____

5. **When you think about your name and the circumstances of your birth, what are your thoughts as it pertains to God?**

_____

_____

_____

_____

_____

_____

_____

_____

_____

_____

_____

_____

Lesson 4

Esther 4:12-17 = Read this portion of Esther that is written in the back of the Course book, and read Ephesians 6:10-18

- **Read <u>Submitting to the Royal Calling</u> in the Course book:**

    1. **What has God called you to do in His royal kingdom?**

    _____

    _____

    _____

    _____

    _____

    _____

    _____

    _____

    _____

    _____

    _____

    _____

    _____

    _____

    _____

    2. **Have you completely answered the call? If yes how? If not why not?**

    _____

    _____

    _____

    _____

    _____

    _____

    _____

    _____

    _____

_____

_____

_____

_____

3. **What does it mean to you that you have been crowned a Queen for such a time as this?**

_____

_____

_____

_____

_____

_____

_____

_____

_____

_____

_____

_____

_____

4. **Do you recall when you first realized you were a Queen and describe when it was and what those feelings were?**

_____

_____

_____

_____

_____

_____

_____

_____

_____

_____

_____

_____

5. **What are some things that have hindered you over the years from walking in who God has called you to be? How does the armor in Ephesians 6 helped in the fight for your anointing?**

_____

_____

_____

_____

_____

_____

_____

_____

_____

_____

_____

_____

Lesson 5

Esther 2:15-18 = Read this portion of Esther that is written in the back of the Course book

- **Read <u>Becoming the King's Selection</u> in the Course book:**

  1. **What have you had to endure to become the King's selection?**

    _____

    _____

    _____

    _____

    _____

    _____

    _____

    _____

    _____

    _____

    _____

    _____

  2. **How has your will sometimes superseded the will of God in your life?**

    _____

    _____

    _____

    _____

    _____

    _____

    _____

    _____

3. How has or does your flesh interfere with your anointing? How can you fight the flesh and win?

_____

_____

_____

_____

_____

_____

_____

_____

_____

_____

_____

_____

4. How can you tell when you are receiving good counsel and when it's just frivolous girl talk disguised as counsel?

_____

_____

_____

_____

_____

_____

_____

_____

_____

_____

_____

_____

5. **What role is the Holy Spirit playing in your anointing? How can you give Him full reign today?**

_____

_____

_____

_____

_____

_____

_____

_____

_____

_____

_____

_____

Lesson 6

Esther 5:1-2 = Read this portion of Esther that is written in the back of the Course book and read 2 Timothy 1:5-7

- **Read <u>Someone Knows My Anointing</u> in the Course book:**

    1. **How has knowledge of your anointing been revealed to you?**

    _____

    _____

    _____

    _____

    _____

    _____

    _____

    _____

    _____

    _____

    _____

    _____

    2. **What are you using to fan your anointing into flame and how is that working for you?**

    _____

    _____

    _____

    _____

    _____

    _____

    _____

    _____

    _____

    _____

3. What are some fears that have trickled in to try to cripple your anointing, and how are you counteracting them?

_____

_____

_____

_____

_____

_____

_____

_____

_____

_____

_____

_____

_____

4. How are you guarding and maintaining the anointing to be Queen?

_____

_____

_____

_____

_____

_____

_____

_____

_____

_____

_____

5. **What circumstances have helped in birthing your anointing, and what must you do to stand strong in it at all times?**

_____

_____

_____

_____

_____

_____

_____

_____

_____

_____

_____

_____

_____

Lesson 7

Esther 4:12-14 = Read this portion of Esther that is written in the back of the Course book and read Job 1:12

- **Read <u>A Treacherous Plot for My Life</u> in the Course book:**

    1. **How does it feel to know that like Job, God has said: have you considered my servant _____? (put your name in the blank)**

    _____

    _____

    _____

    _____

    _____

    _____

    _____

    _____

    _____

    _____

    _____

    _____

    _____

    2. **What is one treacherous thing that has attached itself to you that you need to kill?**

    _____

    _____

    _____

    _____

    _____

    _____

    _____

    _____

3. What risks have you had to take to accomplish your anointing?

_____

_____

_____

_____

_____

_____

_____

_____

_____

_____

_____

4. Who are you blaming for the bad in your life? Why?

_____

_____

_____

_____

_____

_____

_____

_____

_____

_____

_____

5. **Have you chosen the wide easy path or the narrow difficult path to your anointing? Why?**

_____

_____

_____

_____

_____

_____

_____

_____

_____

_____

_____

_____

Lesson 8

Esther 5:1-8 = Read this portion of Esther that is written in the back of the Course book

- **Read <u>Intercession with the King</u> in the Course book:**

1. **When you find yourself in tight spots, like Esther, what do you do first?**

_____

_____

_____

_____

_____

_____

_____

_____

_____

_____

_____

_____

2. **Can you think of times in your life when intercession with the King would be worth dying for? Explain.**

_____

_____

_____

_____

_____

_____

_____

_____

_____

_____

3. If you have ever done so, explain the feeling of boldly entering the throne room and interceding with the King? What is the result?

_____
_____
_____
_____
_____
_____
_____
_____
_____
_____
_____
_____

4. What are some things that hinder you from intercession for others or yourself?

_____
_____
_____
_____
_____
_____
_____
_____
_____
_____
_____

5. **Are you interceding with the King on a daily basis? If yes, how does it impact your life? If not, why not?**

_____

_____

_____

_____

_____

_____

_____

_____

_____

_____

_____

_____

Lesson 9

Esther 4:14-16 = Read this portion of Esther that is written in the back of the Course book

- **Read <u>Anointed for Such a Time as This</u> and <u>Prayer and Fasting Required</u> in the Course book:**

    1. How do you know you are doing your part in God's redemptive plan for your life?

    _____

    _____

    _____

    _____

    _____

    _____

    _____

    _____

    _____

    _____

    _____

    _____

    2. Do you sometimes feel you have wasted your life? How can the phrase "for such a time as this" help you recover?

    _____

    _____

    _____

    _____

    _____

    _____

    _____

    _____

    _____

_____

_____

_____

3. **What major decision have you been confronted with that became the catalyst for you embracing your anointing?**

_____

_____

_____

_____

_____

_____

_____

_____

_____

_____

_____

4. **What role does fasting and praying play in your life? How does it impact your anointing?**

_____

_____

_____

_____

_____

_____

_____

_____

_____

_____

_____

5. **Explain the sacrificial role of prayer and fasting in getting your marching orders from the King.**

_____

_____

_____

_____

_____

_____

_____

_____

_____

_____

_____

_____

Lesson 10

Esther 6:1-3 and 7:1-10 = Read this portion of Esther that is written in the back of the Course book

- **Read <u>A Providence of Hope</u> and <u>The Plot Exposed</u> in the Course book:**

    1. **How does knowing, God providentially cares for you, give you hope?**

    _____

    _____

    _____

    _____

    _____

    _____

    _____

    _____

    _____

    _____

    _____

    _____

    2. **How can being still and quiet help you understand God's providential plan for your life?**

    _____

    _____

    _____

    _____

    _____

    _____

    _____

    _____

    _____

    _____

_____
_____

3. Read the short poem by Ray Pritchard on pages 105-106 in the course book, and explain how it helps you come to grips with God's providence for you.

_____
_____
_____
_____
_____
_____
_____
_____
_____
_____
_____
_____
_____

4. While waiting for your hour of emancipation (release) from the issues and tests of life how do you cope?

_____
_____
_____
_____
_____
_____
_____
_____
_____
_____
_____

_____

_____

5. How are you equipping yourself to be a force to be reckoned with by the enemy of your soul?

_____

_____

_____

_____

_____

_____

_____

_____

_____

_____

_____

_____

Lesson 11

Esther 8:5-8 = Read this portion of Esther that is written in the back of the Course book

- **Read <u>Promoted by God</u> in the Course book:**

  1. **To whom do you look for promotion? Why?**

  _____

  _____

  _____

  _____

  _____

  _____

  _____

  _____

  _____

  _____

  _____

  _____

  2. **How do your earthly tangible promotions compare to your ultimate heavenly promotion by the King of kings?**

  _____

  _____

  _____

  _____

  _____

  _____

  _____

  _____

  _____

  _____

3. How does knowing your promotion could go to someone else if you don't take hold of your anointing motivate you?

_____
_____
_____
_____
_____
_____
_____
_____
_____
_____
_____

4. What have you been promoted by God to do in His kingdom?

_____
_____
_____
_____
_____
_____
_____
_____
_____
_____

_____
_____

5. How are you fulfilling the promotion? What are the losses or gains associated with your promotion?

_____
_____
_____
_____
_____
_____
_____
_____
_____
_____
_____
_____

NOTES

NOTES

NOTES

NOTES

Made in the USA
Middletown, DE
27 November 2021

53527352R00024